The Fish Finger

Sandwich Book

Ideas to spice up your favourite snack

D1332207

Jason Dearn

The Fish Finger Sandwich Book

Published by Lulu.inc

The Self-publishing website.

www.lulu.com

ISBN 978-1-4466-9546-3

Cover photograph By Jason Dearn

Photograph used with permission of Pilotbank UK Ltd

The photograph remains the property of Pilotbank UK Ltd

www.pilotbank.co.uk

admin@pilotbank.co.uk

NOTE:

The information detailed in this book is relayed to the reader in good faith for guidance only.
This book is intended as a humorous look at the fish finger sandwich, cooking, preparation of
food is the responsibility of the reader, and as such, no liability can be accepted for loss or
expense because of information or guidance outlined in this work. The reader should check
any/all-cooking guidelines as outlined on the manufacture's product and is responsible to ensure
that they are followed, including good hygiene standards.
No combos in this book are recommended for resale in a commercial venture.(we wouldn't want
you to go out of business.)

Jason Dearn

The Fish Finger Sandwich Book

By Jason Dearn

Jason Dearn - one of the world's worst selling self-published, in fact, self-published or professionally published authors, was born in the city of Birmingham, in the West Midlands of the United Kingdom, circa 1969.

He was educated, (However, due to him having the knowledge retention of a senile gold fish it is hard to see how) at various schools, in and around the Dudley Borough.

He has never shot to fame, or actually been any good at any thing, but before you let that put you off, just be mindful that he is so poor that by buying this book you will be helping him achieve his life long goal of affording new shoes.

He currently lives in Worcestershire, in a cardboard box, and is frequently moved on by the police from his favourite spot. Luckily, the box is portable.

Needless to say, this is his first book on fish fingers (and possibly his last), and was conceived as a bet, for which he will need to sell at least ten copies to people who do not know him, or feel sorry for him, to win it. Tall orders indeed, considering the word **sell**.

Also By Jason Dearn and Published by Lulu, Inc

<u>Non-fiction self improvement books</u>

The absolute beginners guide to becoming a pilot (2009)

A beginner's guide to becoming a good manager (2010)

An intermediates guide to becoming a good manager (2010)

<u>Non-fiction humorous (allegedly) Fish Finger sandwich books</u>

The Fish Finger Sandwich Book (2010)

Available at Amazon.co.uk , and at all good bookstores, and the odd charity shop no doubt!

Contents

Jason Dearn

The Fish Finger Sandwich Book

Jason Dearn

This book is dedicated to:

Kate – My friend, my soundboard, but most importantly, the person that has banned me from eating any more fish fingers <u>for life</u>!

The two who I cannot name – this one is for you! I just wanted to say thank you for making me feel so welcome!

The Fish Finger Sandwich Book

My thanks to the following people in no particular order

Sujee Newte - Thanks, without your suggestion that this book would make an ideal addition to your friend's downstairs toilet library, it would have never have been written.

The Good peoples of Southampton and South Wales circa 1955. To whom millions of people owe a debt of thanks, for rejecting the Herring Savoury, and endorsing the Fish Finger.

To Clarence Birdseye*, a genius without whom, none of this could have ever been conceived; if in 1928, he had not stumbled upon the idea of fast freezing fish.

(And not forgetting adding breadcrumbs, a detail sometimes forgotten about)

Finally, my mom.

* Please note I am not indorsing a particular brand of frozen fish fingers – but I like them!

Jason Dearn

Chapter one - The basics

Easy Stuff

The Fish Finger sandwich a favourite snack meal of children, students and single men alike. The real question to ask is, "What is the ultimate fish finger sarnie?" Well, if you asked a hundred people (or in this case fifty or so), you would more than likely, get a hundred different answers.

This book has set out to answer that question, well, at least try to allow you to answer that question. Therefore, if you want a simple snack or something a little bit out of the ordinary, then we have it here for you!

In this chapter (and I use the word chapter loosely), we are going to look at the easy stuff to do, the stuff even an average teenager lad could knock up, well, if they ever got up that is...

So let us start at the beginning, with the basic sandwich.

#1 The Basic Sandwich

Ingredients

Bread

Fish fingers

Butter or marg (optional)

Prep

Grill or fry your fish fingers, using the cooking instructions as per the manufactures guide on the packet. Depending on how hungry you are will determine how many fish fingers you prepare. Once cooked through, take the bread out of the packet; butter as required, place the fish fingers on the bread. Cut the completed sandwich as required and eat. *Simple.*

The basic fish finger sandwich should be a no brain-er to make to just about everyone, unless perhaps, you have been living under a rock on mars.
I have included it, because frankly, you just never know if our rock sheltering Martian chum has even seen a fish finger, let a lone consider slapping the beautiful golden delights between two slices of their chosen bread product and calling it a sarnie!

For those of us that have enjoyed the culinary delights of the fish finger sandwich you may want to miss the basic sandwich as a recipe idea and move on. However, a word of note, the basic cooking instructions are fairly consistent in all

Jason Dearn

of the combos, and as such, I will not be listing them again, so if like my kid brother you may forget them, it might be a good time to fold down the corner of the page or write/tattoo them on your arm.

Before starting to list the sandwich ideas, now perhaps is a good time to give you a little history on the fish finger and the sandwich. If you have a life, and therefore don't want to know how the iconic combination of fish finger and sandwich came together, then flick on to page 15 to start you fish finger culinary adventures.

The Fish Finger

Clarence Birdseye, an American biologist, invented the fish finger. He patented the idea in 1927 in the UK, but it took him a further 28 years to produce the idea commercially. First produced in Great Yarmouth in the United Kingdom, the fish finger was manufactured to promote a new way of eating herring, which, until then, had been sold in pickled form – yum!

Before going on sale to the public, Birdseye decided to complete consumer tests; these were taken part by the peoples of Southampton and South Wales. With the fish fingers, being marketed as Cod fish fingers in Southampton, and Herring savouries in South Wales. The surprising findings for the trial, were that the bland control product, i.e. the cod fish fingers, out sold the herring product! Thank God for the good people of South Wales who rejected the herring savoury.

The herring savoury sandwich just doesn't sound so appealing for some reason, and it's a bit of a mouthful to say as well as eat!

So on September 26th, 1955 the fish finger was born, going on sale to the great British public.

Since its introduction, the fish finger has become a firm teatime favourite with Children all over the world, sold in countries such as the USA and France. Being sold in France has surprised me, considering that they have a four-hour lunch break and eat odd things like snails… However, it is pleasing to note that they seem to be catching up with the rest of the world and embracing the humble fish finger as the super food that it is.

In the States, fish fingers are known as Fish Sticks, not entirely sure why, as fish and bits of dead tree doesn't seem such a marketable proposition, but basically it is the same thing so I guess if they want to call them fish sticks who am I to judge! Needless to say, the sticks are equally as popular as in US as they are in the UK.

Some stats for all you anoraks out there, in the UK alone, over one Million fish fingers are eaten every day! I hope that they are eaten in delicious fish finger sandwiches!

The fish fingers are x-rayed whilst in production to find bones!

The Sandwich

The sandwich is eons old, which may come as a bit of surprise to most readers. It is a commonly held myth that the sandwich itself was invented or created by the 4th Earl of Sandwich, which is in fact incorrect. He wasn't out one day riding his horse, shooting pheasants and peasants, when he took hungry and just happened to have a couple of bread slices knocking about.

The earl was actually a big card player, and he needed to eat something whilst at the gaming table. Once others saw what he was eating, they also asked for a "sandwich". The name stuck and as such, any filling between two pieces of bread is now called a sandwich.

The popularity of the sandwich comes from the need of the labour force to eat a quick meal in between shifts at work - the 18th and 19th century version of fast food.

The fish finger sandwich creation date is unknown to me at this time; however, according to the Fish Finger sandwich appreciation society on facebook, it was 1975/76, and it is claimed, to have been invented by Dominic Eldridge and Peter Holder. How true this is a matter of debate, but as the society states, if anyone knows any different then please contact them and they will put it right. Never the less, whoever it was, *they were a bloody genius.* I would be grateful to you, the humble reader, of this fine and important volume of what can only be described as a "classic in the making", if you would all be so bold, as to join the humble society. If for nothing more, than to debate the creation date together (of the fish finger sandwich that is, and not creation itself, which is an entirely different society!). Please don't send your complaints and or law suits to me, as I will have more than likely have left the country, if not the planet on publication. Please direct any, and all, counter challenges on who and when to the society!

13
Jason Dearn

Okay, enough with the history lesson, time to get onto the main event, the sandwich combinations!

The sauces

It would be great to just look down the supermarket shelves and get a hundred or so different sauces, slap it down in alphabetical order and say, "Job done, thanks for buying the book. I'm off to the south of France with my box."

However, that would actually defeat the object of the book in the first place. It would be one short cut too many me thinks.

Nevertheless, for a quick change to the basic sandwich (i.e. Bread-fish fingers-bread) and for those of you that can't arsed to do anything else, I have listed a few suggestions below.

Ketchup – the old chestnut

Fruity or brown sauce

Jerk sauce

Peri peri sauce

Mayo

Salad cream

Sweet chilli dipping (I have been know to wake up the following morning, after a skin full the night before, to find I have eaten these without the bread, i.e. just dipped. Usually to my surprise, I might add!)

Mango chutney

Pickle – not something I would recommend, but if at the end of the month, you only have that or custard left in the cupboard, it is the lesser of two evils!

Custard – for when you have run out of pickle!

Curry sauce

Soy sauce

I could go on, and I am sure the avid reader could suggest further combinations, which if you do feel moved to do so, send them to me on jasondearn@yahoo.co.uk and I'll stick them on the website, or alternatively post to the Face book group. I'm fairly sure they will love you for it!

The easy stuff

This has been the hardest chapter to write! I guess this is for two reasons; firstly, I left this one until last. Never a good idea, as you tend to have run out of steam towards the end of a writing project. Secondly, and more importantly I feel, there are so many fish finger sandwich boxes lying around that I have had trouble finding the lap top!

So the easy stuff, I guess the first one to put down of note is the fish finger, mayo and lettuce combo. This is one of my favourites, I guess because it is, like most sandwiches very easy to make, and the lettuce adds valuable nutrition to my diet…

Jason Dearn

#2 The Fish Finger, Mayo and Lettuce Combo

Ingredients

Fish Fingers (4)

Bread slices (2)

Lettuce leaf (leaves if required)

Mayo

Butter or marg (optional)

Prep

Cook the fish fingers as described, when satisfied that this heat exchange has happened, place on a slice of your chosen bread, apply the mayo (this is important as you need to adhere the lettuce to the fish. Also, it kinda is the critical part of a fish finger, lettuce and mayo sandwich – well, after the fingers and the lettuce that is). Once the mayo is applied, garnish with lettuce, add second slice of bread, and serve.

As I have said this is one of my favourites, easy simple to do, very little effort.

#3 The Fish Finger and Chip Butty

Ingredients

Fish Fingers (4)

Bread slices (2)

Chips (fries for you American readers – Mireille I am sure you are chopping

potatoes as I write!)

Sauce of your choice

Butter or marg (optional)

Prep

This one may test the cooking skill of those of you without any culinary

background, chips tend to involve the cooking of potatoes and not to mention the

slicing of said potatoes. Because of this, and lets be completely honest, I don't

want to get sued for making out that chips are an easy thing to knock up. I am

going to suggest a couple of cheats (if it is good enough for Delia, its good

enough for me!)

Firstly, buy frozen chips; I am told they are widely available now from places

called supermarkets.

On the other hand, as in my case, just nip down the Chippy.

The second cheat tends to have the added hazard of the Greek bloke behind the

counter trying to sell me extra's, like the dodgy pickled eggs and such like – I am

happy to report I do usually get away without buying them, however, Friday

Jason Dearn

nights coming home from the pub I could have bought anything! – You just never know! Anyhow back to the prep..

Cook the Fish Fingers as described until you are happy they are cooked, or the smoke alarm has gone off, place on the bread slice, apply generous amounts of chips (fries), and add the optional sauce of your choice. Top off with the second slice of bread, cut, serve and enjoy!

N.B. One final point to make on this one, you may need to apply pressure to squash the second slice down, dependent upon personal chip application preference.

It is at this point I would like to mention the gang from Madeley. You know who you all are you scamps! I would like to thanks them for the entertaining Monday lunch times we had down in Ironbridge, Shropshire. A world heritage site no less and frankly all the better for the heady debates on the best fish Finger sandwich combo in my humble opinion. Thanks Guys!

#4 The Fish Finger Mash Doorstop

Ingredients

Fish Fingers (4)

Bread slices – must be thick, preferably home cut (2)

Mash Potatoes

Butter or marg (optional)

Now this one is a real bad boy!

Prep

Cut the bread to the appropriate doorstop thickness. The prescribed thickness will depend upon personal taste and regional up bringing – You London wide boys – Cook the fish Fingers, I find when eaten raw, they tend to be a bit crunchy.. Whilst cooking the Golden love bringers, also heat up your store bought mash potatoes. (at this point I feel the urge to ward you off instant potato mash. If I had wanted you to use wallpaper paste, I would have called this combo the fish finger wallpaper doorstop! – keep it real buy the stuff in the carton!)The microwave was invented for this or so I am told.. Once both of the key elements are ready, cut up the fingers – yes cut them up! Lou used to cut everything with scissors, I guess as homage to her you can cut them up with scissors, if you have no scissors to hand or just cant be arsed to cut them up then don't. It does not really matter, but is a nice touch… Apply a huge dollop of mash to the first slice on this doorstop monster creation, then apply your cut up, or not cut up fingers, add second dollop of the mash, and finish off with the crowning glory of the second doorstop. Cut as required and eat. Beauty. *To impress a girl, this is one of those where you could also add some chopped or scissor-ed up chives.*

#5 The Fish Finger Wrap

Ingredients

Fish Fingers (2 per wrap)

Mexican style wraps

Butter or marg (optional)

This one was the subject on much debate - should it really be included in the basic section or should be in the international – or whatever I get round to calling it section. The debate still rages, but as the author it is going in here so tough.

Prep

Cook your breaded wonder sticks and make sure they are piping hot! Take wrap from the packet and place on the plate (for those of you with no experience of the Mexican style wrap, there is no need for a second wrap – unless of course you want two, which will complicate things further as you will need to double the amount of fish fingers you are cooking. For those of you that have already started cooking and are following the prep instructions as you are cooking this is where it could get a. Complicated and b. dangerous as the second set of fish finger you are undoubtedly adding to the pan or the grill will take longer to cook. This could result in one of two things happening and possibly resulting in your death a. by food poisoning due to under cooked fish or b. by raging inferno due to over cooking, forgetting they are under the grill and falling asleep. In this instance, a check of your smoke alarm is recommended. Failing that, just put the fish fingers back in the packet and remember to only get one wrap for next time.)

Place the two fish fingers in the centre of the wrap and then fold the bottom part of the wrap to the centre of the fish fingers. Then fold both sides of the wrap to form the wrap. It is at this point I should remind the reader that if you wanted sauces or to add other stuff, then you should he done this before folding began.

How do you get almost a page of script out of a wrap and two fish fingers – genius – I feel a booker prize coming my way I can tell you!

#6 The Ham and Cheese Fish Finger Wrap

Ingredients

Fish Fingers (2 per wrap)

Mexican style wraps

Grated cheese

Sliced ham

Butter or marg (optional)

Prep

This one is one of those where you need the speed of a ninja and asbestos fingers! Cook your fingers (the fish ones, not your own), whilst they are heating place you wrap on a plate or surface. Take out a slice of ham and place it on the wrap, then take a good hand full of the grated cheese – I use pre bought grated cheese purely for speed – cover the ham with the cheese. Now this is the important bit the fish fingers must be HOT, as you want the heat to melt the cheese! If you are too slow or the cheese refuses to melt, having folded the wrap as per the instruction you can either microwave them or stick them back under the grill! The whole point is that the cheese is melted! This one is a bit annoying at first, but just think of the bread crumby, melty cheesy, fish finger lovely snack at the end of your efforts!!

#7 The Popeye Fish Pitta

Ingredients

Fish Fingers (4 per Pitta)

Pitta Bread

Spinach

Mayo

Curry powder

Prep

This Brutus of a sandwich Idea is my mate Simon's. I have tried this one, and I like it!!! So if you have not already started too, cook your fish fingers! Take out your Pitta bread, and slice open. I like to have already mixed the mayo and curry powder before I cut the pitta, and once the cutting and the mixing is done, I spread a thick layer of the mayo mix on both inside walls of the open pitta. Take the washed spinach leaves and place in the pitta and spoon in any extra mayo mix. Put in the cooked fish "food of the Gods" fingers into the pitta/mayo/spinach envelope and cut, serve and scoff.

"I'm Popeye the sailor man! "Beep beep"" - Quote Becky Batten, Face book 23/11/10

#8 The Fish Finger Omelette Pitta

Ingredients

Fish Fingers (2 per pitta)

Pitta Bread

Cheese omelette (frozen Store bought)

Brown Sauce

Prep

Frozen omelettes were made for this recipe! This is a quickie to do! If Clarence and the Earl had ever sat down for a game of cards, they would be tucking into this sandwich. *Possibly!*

Any ways, to prep this combo, cook the frosty fish fun food and the omelette as per the instructions on the box.   Slice the pitta. When the omelette is cooked, take it from under the grill, slice it open and insert into the prepared pitta. Now I have found that this is the best way to prepare this sandwich, as if you insert the fish fingers into the omelette prior to inserting it into the pitta you'll be in allsorts of bother! So, pop the omelette in the pitta, then take the pitta/omelette construct, and then insert the fingers! Cut as desired and eat.

"Snap", said the Earl. "Bother!" replied Clarence…

#9 The Fish Burger

Ingredients

Fish Fingers (2 per bun)

Burger buns

Cheese

Lettuce

Mayo

Prep

I was stumbling around my local supermarket the other evening – looking for something to take the edge off the 8 pints of beer I had consumed in town before hand. It was during this search I came across the pre made Nucro-wave fish finger bun. Whether it was the beer, or whether it was in the interests of research for you good readers, I bought one!. **What a mistake!** This combo has been included because I am trying to repent for my misguided purchase…

Well, cook the Solid gold yum sticks, put your burger bun on a plate, mayo the inside of the bun, and apply the lettuce to the lower half of the bun. Put the piping hot fish onto the lettuce, apply the cheese and top it off with the sesame seed bun cap.

And almost the same cooking time as the Frankenstein version!!!

#10 The Gemma

Ingredients

Salmon Fish Fingers (4 per slice)

Bread

Beetroot

Lettuce

Horseradish

Butter or marg (optional)

Prep

Now, this is one of the combo's I have not tried. Mainly because I'm not pregnant! *(God I hope Gemma has told everyone – if not oops! Sorry Gem!)* Anyhow, cook the fish fingers, butter your bread, apply generous amounts of store bought beetroot, add salad and horse radish to taste (the jar variety) pop on the fish fingers and cut, serve and eat.

Gem, I have amended this combo, as I am fairly sure that toothpaste isn't to everyone's taste. However, readers it is up to you!

#11 The Cowboy

Ingredients

Fish Fingers (2 per wrap)

Wraps

Beans

BBQ sauce

Prep

This one is a bit messy. Nevertheless, it is a nice combo, the beans just work, even if you do need a bib to eat it! Cook the Frozen wonder fingers! Open the beans and cook as per instructions. I use those microwave pots, it is just easy to manage the timings and the quantities, not to mention the lack of washing up.. Get out your wrap apply any BBQ sauce to the wrap and place your fish in the centre.. Fold the wrap around the fish fingers! DO NOT ADD THE BEANS AT THIS POINT! Make sure you have wrapped it first! (When wrapping, leave enough room for your beans.) Take out the micro pot beans and carefully pour in the amount you require per wrap! Eat and enjoy!

I always add cheese to the beans once they are poured in, but this is not a requirement, just my personal taste!

#12 The Salmon mash roll

Ingredients

Salmon Fish Fingers (2 per Roll)

Bread rolls (any type to taste)

Mayo

Chilli powder

Prep

When the salmon fish finger made its first appearance in stores, I was

apprehensive at best! I felt that they debased the whole fish finger being a

universal food giant in the culinary landscape, making it more appealing to the

middle classes etc..lol But I guess I am a convert! They taste damn fine..

This combo is fairly straightforward, cook the wonderful salmon lovelies,

meanwhile mix in chilli powder, to taste, with the mayo, spread the mix thickly on

your roll of choice. Once cooked, mash your fingers and pop on the rolls, lid, cut

and consume..

Please note; for those of you expecting this to contain mash potato, it doesn't -

Sorry

Jason Dearn

#13 The Posh Brekkie Bagel

Ingredients

Salmon Fish Fingers (2 per bagel)

Bagels

An egg per bagel

Mayo (add horse radish if you like)

Black pepper

Prep

Cook the fish! Cut the bagel, mix the mayo with the horseradish and apply to the newly toasted bagel! As the fish is cooking, start to cook the egg – Fried – nothing else with do! When both egg and fish have cooked to your taste, apply to the toasted and mayo-ed bagel, season with pepper as required. Top it off and enjoy!! This is one of my favourite breakfast finger wonder meals! Yum!!

#14 The Full Box Fat Boy!

Ingredients

Fish Fingers (10 per sandwich)

Bread (3 slices per sandwich)

What ever else you want to!

Prep

The full box fat boy - This is dedicated to Mr Kellam. Thanks for this one, I was very happy to hear about the urban myth surrounding this one! Basically, the myth is that the fish finger manufactures' put 10 fish fingers in their basic entry so you can get two basic sandwiches out of them. I.e. five fish fingers per sandwich, four in the horizontal and one in the vertical... This combo is inspired by that myth. So, cook the entire box of your ten golden happiness injectors. You will need three slices of your desired bread. Cook the entire box of fish sticks. (make sure it a ten pack box, a bumper pack could be a bit more than most people can handle!) Prep the bread how ever you like. Toasted, plain, buttered... add any thing else you would like; sauces etc... place 5 of the fingers in the four and one configuration, add the next slice and repeat. Then add the top and wolf this fat boy down. (If by some remote chance, you do cook 36 fish fingers whilst preparing this one you can either add extra bread and form a Scooby style sandwich, or invite some friends round. The latter being the option less likely to involve a stomach pumping or a crash diet.)

Perhaps this sandwich is best suited to the aficionado with a bigger appetite.

Chapter Two – Traditional

This our second chapter on fish finger sandwich combinations deals with traditional ideas adapted to fit on a sandwich and use fish fingers! As you will be able to tell from the above statement, I have put years of research into writing this definitive work on the fish finger sandwich, and as such, you will be delighted and inspired. – Yeah right.

At this stage in your mastery of the dark arts of the fish finger sandwich, I have stuck to plain common-all-garden white square sliced bread, as the combos that come in later chapters explore the exciting world of other bread products. Wow, I know!

As we press on through the book, the combo's will get a little more adventurous and demanding, in terms of culinary skill required. I like to think that this book, as part of its remit, will develop the lost generations of students and single men's food preparation skill to such an extent, that local fast food joints could struggle to survive! At the very least, waking up to a face full of kebab on your pillow may well be a thing of the past. Trust me, for those of you that have yet to go through this horror, I have saved you from an embarrassment worse than waking up next someone and trying to sneak out before dawn because you cannot remember their name. It is that bad! (For those of you that have never sneaked out, it is as bad as waking up with a face full of kebab – this could go on for hours! Let us move on.)

#15 The Fish Finger Kedgeree

Ingredients

Fish Fingers (2 per slice)

Eggs

Milk

Frozen Peas

Rice

Bread

Paprika or curry powder

Prep

I like to think that this must be a first – Fish Fingers for breakfast (fish finger producers everywhere will be rejoicing at this bad boy!)! Kedgeree is a traditional breakfast meal with its origins being from the time of the British Raj in India. It is a very Scottish breakfast, and a damn fine alternative to oats! I guess after eating oats, cardboard would be an evolutionary step on the breakfast scale.

Anyhow, how to cook it. First, and you maybe beginning to see a pattern here in my writing, cook your fish fingers. Whilst doing that, either boil or scramble some eggs. I will always go with the scramble option… chuck in a handful of frozen rice and peas into the pan, and add the beaten egg and milk mix. Once both eggs and fish are cooked, transfer to a dish and break up the eggs and fish with a fork. The bread at this stage should be toasting in the toaster. When the fish – egg combo is beaten within an inch of its life add curry powder or paprika to taste and serve on the buttered toast – Well worth the effort! A guaranteed wife pleaser!

Please do not mention me in any divorce petitions – I didn't do it!

#16 The Rebecca Scottish Special

Ingredients

Fish Fingers (2 per slice)

Bread (Crusty or French stick – she was very specific)

Béarnaise Sauce

Eggs

Prep

My mate Bex suggested this combo to me, bear in mind that Bex is a genius in the kitchen, having run gastro pubs for about 8 years. Now Bex can make anything out of anything, so I am thankful that she has kept it simple!!

This is a breakfast, again from Scotland, and is a variation on classic eggs Benedict, firstly cut your crusty bread! Toast the bread and apply butter. The Fish should be cooking using your preferred method. You will need to poach the egg – for those of you who are strangers to the stove, this does not mean that you raid the local hen house at midnight. It requires you to boil water on the stove, and crack an egg into the boiling water! By now the toast should be done. Add the fish fingers to the bread, fish out the egg and plonk it on the top. Pour over your Béarnaise sauce and serve – this is gorgeous. Thank you Rebecca!

#17 The Full English Tower

Ingredients

Fish Fingers (2 per sandwich)

Bread (3 slices per sandwich)

Potato Waffles

Tomato Puree

Smoked Back Bacon (2 rashers per sandwich)

Eggs (1 per sandwich)

Sauce (variety is a personal choice)

Prep

This is a full meal or a big snack for us on the fatter side of life! The prep for this one is a little more complex, as there is a lot going on! Cook your fish fingers under the grill whilst also sharing it with the waffle, fire up the frying pan and fry your bread! Yeah baby! Fried bread! Once done, start to cook your bacon. Then fry your egg. Assemble: take one slice of the deliciously fried bread, add the bacon, the puree and the waffle. Put on the middle slice of fried bread. On the second tier add your fish fingers then the egg and top off with the final slice of fried bread! Cut in down the middle and serve.

N.B. This must be washed down with the biggest mug of tea that you can muster!

#18 Surf and Turf

Ingredients

Fish Fingers (2 per sub style roll)

Sub or torpedo rolls

Very Thin frying steak

An onion

Scampi

Horseradish

Salad garnish to taste

Prep

This one is a take on my standard order at my local gastro pub! The usual stuff first, cook your fish! Take out your scampi and deep fry this as per the instructions. The steak also needs to be started, but that is dependant on how you like, I like mine cooked to a point where a good vet could bring it back. But that is my choice! Sweat the onions in a pan. Cut your subs down the middle and spread on a liberal amount of horseradish. Lay in your steak and onions, Put on your cooked scampi and fish fingers, I tend to mash these, but again it is a person thing! Then garnish to your personal taste with the salad,

#19 The Leakey-leek Salmon Special.

Ingredients

Salmon Fish Fingers (2 per slice)

Bread

Leeks

Crème fraiche

Frozen peas

Salt and Black pepper

Prep

This combo is unashamedly dedicated to team Leake! Thanks for all of your friendship, the good times, and encouragement with this book!

Cook the salmon fish fingers. Slice the leeks up very thinly. Put the peas, the leeks and two spoons of crème fraiche into a bowl and microwave for about 40 seconds – the peas should be cooked. Place the fish on the bread of your choice, and the spoon on the crème fraiche mixture on the top and season to taste! For something extra just add tarragon (must be fresh). Enjoy! xxx

This one should only ever be cut with Scissors!

#20 The Salmon and Sundried Tomato Wrap

Ingredients

Salmon Fish Fingers (2 per wrap)

Wraps

Chopped bay leaf

Sundried Tomatoes

Onion

Black pepper

Fresh basil

Prep

A very simple wrap, cook the fish fingers, mean while chop the onion and warm with the sundried toms, the bay leaf. Once cooked and warmed, place the fingers in the wrap, pour over the sun-dried toms, a twist of black pepper and add the basil, fold your wrap and serve. Lovely.

#21 The Curried Fish Finger Naan Fold

Ingredients

Fish Fingers (2 per naan)

Naan Bread

Cucumber

Onion

Riata sauce

Curry Powder

Prep

I was slumped in a chair in my local curry house recently when this idea came to me. I had been out, and frankly, may have had one too many, or was it the air after I came out of the pub... Needless to say, I ended up in a curry house face down in a chicken balti, talking drunk talk about how I still loved my ex girlfriend and that if we ever got back together planets would align and it would signify world peace etc etc. Needless to say, we didn't, it hasn't and frankly, it may have actually averted world war three! Anyhow, back to the story...

I was kind of mid book at the face-down-in-the-balti hallelujah moment, when I realised I might be able to come up with some kind of Indian styled sandwich centred on the beautiful fish delights.

That flash of genius resulted in two things;

1. It got me thrown out of the curry house. A long and uncomfortable story, which I do not fully remember*. *Fortunately.*

2. The combo listed below. Enjoy!

First off, cook the mandatory fish fingers. They need, once cooked and turned once, to be dusted with the curry powder or paprika, then allowed to be finished cooking!

Meanwhile chop up the cucumber and onion in to small cubes and mix with the sauce, Indian restaurant styley. Warm your naan bread as prescribe on the packet. Once warmed, spread on your sauce mix, and add your devilled fish fingers and fold your naan! Inspired!

A note to clear up any confusion with any of my exe's, the face down in the curry house experience is my main way of getting over you! Needless to say, it has happened a lot!

#22 lemon and Coriander

Ingredients

Fish Fingers (2 per Bap)

Cheese topped baps

Lemon and coriander Sauce

Salad as required

Prep

Do I really need to tell you to cook the fish fingers again? If I do, as you may have forgotten this - cook the fish fingers! Okay?

Slice your cheese-topped baps and spread on the lemon and coriander sauce, you can butter the bap, if required, a personal taste thing. Once the fish is cooked, yes cooked! Apply to the bap, add any salad you require and eat.

#23 Watercress and Stilton

Ingredients

Fish Fingers (2 per slice)

Bread

Stilton Cheese

Watercress

Prep

Grill, fry or dare I say it, microwave your fish, take out your bread and garnish with your watercress leaves. Add your cooked fish fingers and crumble your stilton on top and apply the other slice of bread. Cut and eat.

Alas, I haven't really got a back story for this one. I guess I just like stilton and watercress as combination, but I guess you couldn't really pour on a tin of soup and call it a sandwich! God knows I have tried!

#24 the Hollandaise

Ingredients

Fish Fingers (2 per slice)

French Stick Bread

Hollandaise

Butter to taste

Prep

Now Hollandaise sauce is one of the classics from French cooking! It is ridiculously hard to make and as such, I suggest you nip down the shop and buy a pot of the premade stuff! Apparently, it is so named to please the King of Holland when he made a trip to the Frenchies some time in the past, So if that's the case, if its fit for a king it good enough for us. A line of thinking which may have upset the French peasants once or twice before. Eh Marie-Anne?

Enough with the history, cook your golden breaded love rods, and tear and slice your French stick. Then take your hollandaise sauce mix, the pre-bought stuff, or if you are brave enough, the homemade sauce. Butter your bread, apply the cooked fish and pour over the sauce mix. *Bon appetite.*

Chapter Three – Toasty's

Some of you may be surprised to learn that this entire section of the book is given over to the toasting of the prescribed bread that you place around the super foodstuff that are Fish Fingers. I thought the title was a little ambiguous but we went with never the less. Therefore, for those of you who have been surprised? *Sorry.*

To enable you to continue reading this chapter it is recommended that you confirm (we just want to avoid disappointment at some later cooking stage) that you have one or more of the following cooking appliances

1. a toaster

2. a sandwich toaster

3. a grill

My editor, who for some reason did not even want to be paid for this work, (let alone be credited with it), did mention that perhaps we should have mentioned the appliance issue earlier in the book. However, I told him or her (not that they are confused, they just did not want to take any chances on being identified) that they were over reacting. Therefore, John you're over reacting, consider yourself told!

#25 The Fish Finger Pizza inspired Toasty

Ingredients

Fish Fingers (2 per slice)

Bread

Cheese

Tomato Puree

Mixed Herbs

* You will need a grill for this badass combo.

Prep

Like most of the sandwiches in this book, this really is simple to prepare. Firstly switch on the grill – you would be surprised how many times one can forget the basics... Once the grill is at the right temperature, or in my case, orange...put your Fish Fingers under to cook. Once they are cooked through, place your chosen bread under the grill, toast only one side. Once the toasting of the one side is complete, take out the single side toasted bread and start to apply the tomato puree to the non-toasted side.

Cut up the hot fish fingers and sprinkle lovingly on to the newly pureed side and then whack a load of cheese on the top and bang it back under the grill until the cheese is melted, take out and wolf it down.

You can also use a store bought pizza base for this, but if I'm honest I couldn't be arsed, so I just used bread...

Ps you can also stick herbs on it too in case anyone was wondering..

#26 The Rabid Fish Finger Cheese Toasty

Ingredients

Fish Fingers (2 per slice)

Bread

Cheese

Worcestershire Sauce

*You will need a grill for this funkster!

Prep

The title of this one suggests that perhaps I am asking you to tackle the fish

fingers that have gone bad.. Maybe hand to hand combat as you wrestle them

out of the box.. Alas, it is actually a play on words and is more like Welsh rarebit.

The cooking of this one is not dissimilar to the pizza toasty, just don't stick on the

puree, and add the Worcestershire sauce when you take it out. This one is one of

my stable fav's...yum!

#27 The Sweet Pineapple Toasty

Ingredients

Fish Fingers (2 per slice)

Bread

Pineapple chunks

Sweet chilli dipping Sauce

You will need a sandwich toaster for this one

Prep

Warm up you toasted sandwich maker! This is important – Cook the fish fingers first! – butter the bread so it doesn't stick to the sandwich maker!! Once the fingers are golden, place the bread in the sandwich maker, spoon on the sauce add the pineapple and the fish fingers, one per side, place on the second piece of bread, close the lid and toast.

A word of warning. Do not eat this one straight from the sandwich maker, or you will burn your mouth! This one is a firm favourite of mine. Sweet, sticky and lovely!!

#28 The Salmon Broccoli Cheese Melt

Ingredients

Salmon Fish Fingers (2 per slice)

Bread

Cheese

Broccoli

you need to grill this open sandwich

Prep

This melt is a toast-based open sandwich, to prepare firstly boil some water for the broccoli. Unless of course you want to micro wave it! Lol

Cook the fish fingers, whilst also toasting the bread on one side only.

Once the broccoli is tender, and the fish fingers are cooked, break them up into chunky pieces and place on the untoasted side of your bread. Add you broccoli and sprinkle with grated cheese. Then place the toasty back under the grill – till the cheese is melted, take out and eat! Superb!

#29 The Sweetcorn And Mayo Toasty

Ingredients

Fish Fingers (2 per slice)

Bread

Sweetcorn

Mayo

Prep

This is another one of the combo's that requires the fish fingers to be mashed! I can hear the purists now scream at their copies of the book saying,"how dare he suggest this obscene action of violence!" To the purists – Tough, it tastes great. So, heat the fish until cooked, take out your white sliced bread and butter if required. Drain your sweet corn and mix in with a couple of tablespoons of mayo. Once the fish is cooked, mash them into the mayo sweet corn mix. Once mashed and mixed, spread the mixture over your bread and add the all-important second slice. *Yum!*

Ps. Don't forget to toast your bread!

#30 The Fish Finger Club

Ingredients

Fish Fingers (4 per slice)

Bread

Bacon, lettuce and tomato

Mayo

Prep

This is a combo unashamedly based on the club sandwich! A club sandwich for those readers who are unfamiliar is a triple layered, toasted sandwich, usually with turkey or chicken on the first layer filling and then bacon, lettuce and tomato on the second layer filling. It is claimed to have been invented in the late 19th century in the New York gambling clubs – Clarence and the Earl would be most proud to finally see this combination now appear! This one is for you guys!

If you hadn't guessed already we are going to replace the turkey with fish fingers! So, cook the breaded wonder stuff, and start to toast three slices of bread. Cook your bacon, I grill mine, but you can cook yours how ever you like. Once the toast, bacon, and fish are ready, assemble the fish on the bottom slice of toast, having used the mayo to coat the bread. Add the second slice, then apply more mayo and the lettuce bacon and sliced tomato if required, and then top off with the last slice of toast.

Traditionally, the club is cut into four and held together with cocktail sticks, I am not going to stipulate that, but in the interest of history, I do!

In addition, you need to cut this one with scissors .

#31 Sweet and Sour

Ingredients

Fish Fingers (2 per slice)

Crusty Bloomer style Bread

Sweet and sour sauce

Noodles and dipping sauce

* Dependent upon the sauce you buy, add mini sweet corn and pineapple

Prep

The classic oriental dish! Sweet and sour prawns are a classic Chinese dish, so why can't we have a classic using fish fingers? Okay, not your first thought.. As with every combination in this book, I have stayed away from the "making from scratch" methods of cooking. This is supposed to be fun and quick to do.. But if your so minded, please feel free to browse the inter web for a suitable recipe and make it yourself! Anyhow, Cook your fishy delights as per the instructions, open the sweet and sour sauce packet and heat as required! If it has no veg or other lumps in it consider adding your own, such as pineapple and baby sweet corn etc.. you know what I mean... I just buy the pre done stuff – its easier! Once the fish is cooked break up and add to the sauce which should be heated by now. Mix well, and spoon some of the mixture onto your bread and top off with the other slice.

Serve with noodles – the micro ping type and a dipping sauce! Enjoy!

#32 The Caesar

Ingredients

Fish Fingers (2 per slice)

Bread

Croutons

Romaine lettuce

Caesar salad dressing

Worcestershire Sauce

Black pepper

Prep

It is a widely held belief that the Caesar salad was invented in the twenties by a Mexican descendant living in the States call Caesar Cardini. On July the 4th, 1924 to be exact! *I am not going to get you to make the dressing from scratch, well you can if you want, but you will need to go look it up – just buy the dressing!* The sandwich consists of a toasted bread base, the cooked fish fingers of course, with a layer of the romaine lettuce. Cut up your cooked fish fingers and scatter on the lettuce along with the croutons (may be a bit of bread overkill, but just consider it a second slice!) Then add the salad dressing to taste and season and finish off with the Italian style cheese (or parmesan if you can afford it) *A big Thank you to Caesar!*

#33 The Seafood Special

Ingredients

Fish Fingers (1 per slice)

Salmon Fish Fingers (1 per slice)

Bread

Prawns

Lettuce

Seafood sauce

Paprika

Prep

Cook both the types of fish finger. Again, you can either toast the bread or have it plain. I prefer toasted myself, but that is just me. Take the seafood sauce and mix in the pre cooked prawns. Shred your iceberg (lettuce make sure is not wet) and spread on your bread, cut up your fish fingers into smallish chunks and mix with the seafood sauce/prawn ensemble, then when well mixed pour on the sandwich. For those of you old enough to remember the seventies, this is a take on the prawn cocktail – with out the glass. Tastes good mind.

Oh, before you eat.. Add the paprika to taste

#34 The Chilli Ginger Dipper

Ingredients

Fish Fingers (2 per slice)

Bread

Ginger and chill relish

*You will need a sandwich maker for this combo!

Prep

A nice easy one to finish the toasted stuff. This involves a toasted sandwich maker, so if you don't have one, the seafood special is the last one you can make from this section! Anyhow, cook the fish sticks, fish finger or however they are marketed were you are from, as per the instructions on the box. Butter your bread so it doesn't stick to your sandwich maker (if haven't got one, why are you still reading?) The fish should be cooked before you put them in the sandwich maker, I cut them up but you can put them in whole. Take a tablespoon of the ginger sauce, put on the bread, add the second slice, and start to toast the sandwich in your toasted sandwich maker.

Easy!

Chapter Four – Exotic

combos

The exotic chapter is to try to bring in an international flavour to the humble fish finger sandwich. I have tried to list some of the major cultures in this section, taking the themes from the culture and twisting it all up with fish fingers…

This has been a bit of a creative challenge, and mid way through my diet of fish fingers, I am quite please for the change of style. I have still managed to stuff in my second favourite food group – cheese – but there is a lot of healthier alternatives to some of the basics I have already listed!! I guess I have had to be quite subjective with the cultures, for example try as I might, I couldn't find anything that didn't include frozen seal from the Eskimo culinary style, and because I think you may struggle to get the ingredients at your local Market I have left it out. But if any of you do find a supplier of seal etc.. let me know and I'll saddle up the huskies and get on down to the local igloo…

I guess for those of you that are excited by culture, you can now do it from the comfort of your kitchen table, saving yourself a fortune in airfare and not using up your carbon foot print allowance to boot – Green and cultured.. I am a genius.

#35 The German One!

Ingredients

Fish Fingers (2 per slice)

Rye Bread, sour dough or pumpernickel if you can get it!!

An apple – cox's

Sour cream – pot of

Horseradish

Sugar and salt

Prep

Toast your bread and start the fish finger transformation process, cook then cut up. Meanwhile, mix the cream, horseradish and grated apple together in a pan. Adding sugar and salt to taste. When warmed through, add the mashed or cut up fingers to the sour mix and then pour over the rye bread – *guten appétit!*

This recipe came from a traditional Ash Wednesday baked fish dish, served in Germany. I chose it because I didn't want to use the old chestnut of sauerkraut.. Just to avoid the bad jokes and a possible international incident!

#36 The Polish One

Ingredients

Fish Fingers salmon variety (2 per slice)

Bread – Polish sour dough bread, if you can get it, rye bread will do.

Cucumber

Asparagus

Red onion

Red pepper

Lemon vinaigrette

Dill

Prep

Grill the salmon fish delights and toward the end, grill the asparagus till crunchy.

Mean while mix up the dill and the vinaigrette and spread thinly on the rye bread.

Slice up the cucumber and place on the bread. Chop up the red onion and

pepper. Place the salmon and the asparagus on to the bed of cucumber and

garnish with the onion and the pepper drizzle with the remaining vinaigrette.

Jason Dearn

#37 The New Yorker!

Ingredients

Fish Fingers (2 per bagel)

Bagels

Philadelphia style cheese

Prep

I love bagels, bagels on there own, bagels with bacon, *bagels, bagels, bagels*!

Toast the bagels and cook your Fish Fingers, lash on a load of the cheese on the toasted and split bagel, the stick on the fish. Cut. Scoff. Divine!

#38 The French One

Ingredients

Fish Fingers (2 per slice)

French stick

Brie

Garlic paste

Garlic mayo

Olive Oil

Snails pureed – only kidding…lol

Prep

This one is very nice, mainly because I love French brie… So, slice up your French stick, the shallower the angle the better you want about 30 degrees to the horizontal, the longer the better. Once cut, apply the garlic paste and some olive oil. Toast the bread briefly!!! Oh, forgot to mention, put the fish under the grill while you are cutting the bread – silly me, how could I forget??? I must be getting repetitive *brain* injury!! Once the bread is lightly toasted and the fingers are cooked, Mash them in a bowl with some garlic mayo and apply to the toast. Cut generous amounts of brie, apply to the top, and heat the cheese until melted under the grill. ALLOW COOLING – being an impatient plum I went straight in with this one and burned the roof of my mouth – chump…

Ps if you can get pureed snail you can apply to your own taste. However, I would recommend commercial bought puree.. I Don't want the British Organisation of Lets "Love Our Crazy Kritters" Society (B******S for short) taking out a Jihad on my ass 'cause you are all liquidising the garden variety!!!

#39 The Burger Tower!

Ingredients

Fish Fingers (2 per bun)

Hamburger buns

Cheese,

Bacon (two rashers per bun)

Burger (1 per bun)

Prep

This is a take on the hamburger, I could say it was inspired by American cuisine; however, it is more about what I had left at the end of the week in the freezer before I went shopping! So, it has a hamburger in it and that loosely makes it American inspired okay? Happy? It is my book and so here it stays!

Anyhow, cook the fish, your burger and your bacon, slice your bun and when the fish, bacon and burger are cooked, assemble with the burger first, the bacon second and finally the fish. Top off with a cheese slice, add salad, relish, mustard or onions as per your preference and put the bun lid on, and enjoy.

#40 The Italian Slipper

Ingredients

Fish Fingers

Ciabatta bread

Can of chopped tomatoes (Bruschetta mix)

Garlic paste or the spread stuff in a jar

Olive oil

Dried basil

Prep

This one is all about the bread! You need to cut the bread up into half-inch slices. Coat the bread with olive oil and a generous amount of the garlic paste – you can use garlic gloves and rub it into the bread – but that is far too much like hard work. Once done, toast the bread on the one garlic and oiled side only! Heat up the Bruschetta/tomatoes and cook off the fish fingers. Once this is all cooked, cut or mash up the fish fingers and apply a spoon of the mix to the bread. Then spoon on some of the Bruschetta mix and garnish with the basil. *Grande!*

ps. This is called the slipper because "Ciabatta" is Italian for slipper. Not just tasty, but educational too!! lol

#41 The Belfast Belter

Ingredients

Fish Fingers (2 per pancake)

Batter mix

Colcannon

Raw potato

Prep

The Belfast belter is an Irish inspired idea, unusually for a book about fish finger sandwiches; there is no bread in this combo.

Take you batter mix and follow the instructions on the packet. If you want to make from scratch then do it, but for me a 7p packet of basic batter mix does the job. Once mixed, pour into a warmed and oiled frying pan. Take your potato and grate it raw into the batter mix whilst in the pan. In the mean time, cook your fish fingers and warm up your store bought colcannon (Irish mash made with either kale or cabbage and sometimes leeks) Check your pancake and turn or flip when ready. Once the fish, colcannon and the pancake are ready. Spread on your colcannon, and break up the fish and fold the pancake. This is great on a cold day!

#42 The Gentry

Ingredients

Salmon Fish Fingers (1 per muffin)

English muffins

Cucumber

A sprig of mint

Mayo

Prep

This is to be taken with afternoon tea! Cook your salmon Fish Fingers, and slice up your cucumbers. The muffins are to sliced into two and spread some of the mayo on the underside. Adorn with the cucumber and then add your cooked salmon fish fingers and add the lid to the muffin.

You can toast your muffins if your wish. Again, it is a personal taste.

This one is the perfect sarnie for watching the tennis old bean!

#43 The Sicilian

Ingredients

Fish Fingers (2 per sub)

Sub Rolls

Italian style grated cheese

Basil leaves

Cherry toms

Balsamic vinegar

Mustard

Mayo

Sliced black olives (optional)

Prep

Cut the sub rolls down the middle. Start the frozen manna under the grill. This combo does requires a little of mixing, so put a dollop of mayo in a mixing bowl add a splash of balsamic and a tea spoon of the mustard and mix it all up. Once mixed, apply it to the sub roll. Then put the basil leaves into the roll, put in your fish fingers add the cherry toms, sliced olives on top, finish off with the cheese, and melt if required.

Now this will separate the Mafiosi from the boys!

Chapter Five – The down

right odd combos

This final chapter is a voyage into the unknown, others have suggested most of these combo's to me. I have tried them (except the diet one), and they are edible – mostly.

I guess this chapter is for the die-hard devotee – the Bruce of fish finger connoisseurs.

The people that will try anything, anywhere, anyhow! Kinda the Jackass of the fish finger sandwich fraternity.

Most of these are experimental – so go experiment! Enjoy the art of putting stuff together. I also want to hear about them. As I have already stated, and will again, I will write another volume, or maybe two – all of which will be your idea's, your combos and your disasters. Nevertheless, that is what for me has made this project worthwhile – let us have fun! With everything else that is going on, why not have some fun!

Let us do the weird…

#44 The Leigh Pea

This suggestion was given to me by a chum of mine called Leigh, she and I work together and were talking about the life changing volume of work that is "The Fish Finger Sandwich" book, when she told me of her own personal favourite!

Ingredients

Fish Fingers (2 per slice)

Bread

Peas

Salad cream

Prep

When I got home after speaking to Leigh, I attempted this one, mainly because I was hungry. I had the stuff knocking around in the back of the freezer and thought, "why not". It was a bit of a voyage, as she didn't give the assembly instructions so I HAVE WINGED IT! Leigh, if I have it wrong then Let me know!! Lol

Cook the fish fingers, cut your bread and microwave your peas. I used mushy; I guess they have more of an adhesive nature than regular pea's. Picture picking up your sandwich and have most of it fall in your lap! After all, it is a devil of a job getting the pee stains out of the crotch… oops, I meant *pea*. The bread is coated with salad cream, lashings of it! Then the puree pea mix is applied and then the fish sticks atop of the peas. Simple.

It is not as bad as it sounds, an acquired taste me thinks. *Has gotta be better than custard at the end of the month.*

#45 The Jimbo Geordie Special – *mun*

(You need your Geordie accent for this one)

Ingredients

Fish Fingers (2 per Stottie)

Stottie

Pease pudding

Prep

Jimmy Robson I told you I would include this Geordie inspired combo!! For the rest of the planet, Jim and I discussed the book before I even cooked a fish finger; he asked that I put a mention and a combo in for him. Well Jim, here it is. Hope it was worth the wait!

Okay, first things first, open a bottle of Newcastle brown ale, drink. Cook your fish fingers and warm up your Pease pudding. Pease pudding is widely available. Drink another Newcastle brown. Spread the Pease pudding on the stottie (a large bun). Drink another Newcastle brown ale, by this now you will be opening then with your bear hands – the Geordie way. Apply your fish fingers, top of with the other half of the stottie, and enjoy.

It is not only the fish that feels battered after that one! I need a lie down.

#46 The Boxing Day Savoury Saviour

Ingredients

Fish Fingers (2 per slice)

Bread

Cranberry stuffing

Prep

Two things that I used to hate;

1. Boxing day

2. Stuffing

The reasons for these are that one, I feel stuffed on boxing day and just fancy a quick and easy meal after picking at the all the Christmas dinner left over's.

Two, I hated stuffing with my dinner! (this changed when Lou encouraged me to try some – she only like the really well done bits, not the soft under cooked mush in the middle – since then I have been hooked!)

I guess this one is an acquired taste, but it is one I'll be sitting down too this boxing day tea time whilst watched Dr who on my sky plus box... Mainly because mom and my other relatives will be watching the 18 hours of corrie, east enders and god know what else whilst I am round theirs on Christmas day – but that is for another book.

Anyhow, cook the frozen golden wonders, get hold of the left over stuffing – and spread on your bread. Now you can either toast or go with regular, I prefer toasted. Put the fish on and top off with the other slice. Ho Ho Ho!

#47 The Black Goatee

Ingredients

Fish Fingers (2 per slice)

Bread

Goats Cheese

Black pudding sliced

You will need a grill for this one!

Prep

This is for people with a palette for strong flavours, or no palette at all! This isn't one of mine by the way, as I tend to projectile vomit at the thought of goats cheese – I have a bucket here as I tap this one out in the sea of fish finger boxes! Nevertheless, to continue, for those of you who may be interested in this one! I will soldier on!

Cook your converted fish brick lets, as per the instructions or to your own taste – you may like the crunch of them al Dante.. There is no accounting for taste.. Meanwhile, cut your goats cheese into thin slices, and your black pudding into think slices, place the black pudding in the frying pan and cook to taste, on the first cooked (once you have turned them) side, place the goats cheese and allow the second side cook to melt the cheese, once ready, bung everything on the bread and eat. The things I have done for this book eh? Madness… *and vomit*!

#48 The Marmalade and Dill wrap

Ingredients

Fish Fingers (2 per wrap)

Wrap

Dill

Prep

I have to admit that this sounds gross! But, give it a try as the flavours are a classic combination for fish dishes!!

Cook the fish, take a tablespoon of marmalade and add dill to taste. Once you have mixed the dill and preserve, then spread it thickly on your waiting wrap. Add your cooked fish and serve! I you think about it this book is about making something from nothing – or to put it another way – not spending any money in the last week before payday! This bad boy is up there with the best of them!!!

#49 The Sweet Fish Finger Pancake

Ingredients

Fish Fingers (1 per pancake)

Batter mix

Custard

Ice cream

Prep

I will be amazed if anyone actually sends a picture of this one to the website!

This one really is gross!

This combo was cobbled together after a night on the beer. The next day I woke up in the bathroom face down next to the toilet – need I say more! The talk was of fish finger sandwiches and the unusual! I guess it must have been sometime after Matt had aired as the new Doctor, as on the sheet of beer mat I had held in my hand all night; the scrap of paper contained the phrase, "that bloke on the tele did custard!"

So I did. Moreover, it was rank! However, I ate every bit.

Anyhow back to the prep, I cooked the fish, knocked up a pancake using the batter mix I found in the back of the cupboard. Cut the top bit of a Cornetto(I ate the cornet bit – it was very nice) and shoved that on the pancake, poured on some heated custard and then whacked on the fish finger and rolled the whole thing up.

This one tasted different.. Not one I would recommend – more of a warning… If someone knocks up a fish finger trifle, then I will take my hat off to him or her! (Also, I'll put it in the next book! Just go to the website to submit the instructions and the photo!)

#50 The Sweet Marmite Bagel

Ingredients

Fish Fingers (2 per bagel)

Bagel

Cheese slices

Marmite

Honey

Prep

This is one of those that you will either love or hate! I love marmite, so this is a no

brainer for me!! Cook your frozen joy bringers, again, as per the instructions or

just how you like them… in the mean time, toast your bagel and mix one table

spoon of honey to half a tea spoon of marmite. When the bagel is toasted, thinly

spread the sweet marmite combo on the bagel and put on the fish. Add you

cheese slice and your lid! Happy days!

#51 The Diet One!

Ingredients

Fish Fingers (1 per sandwich)

Bread – that nimble stuff.

Cottage cheese

Lettuce

Prep

This is the last combo in the book, I know, I know you are gutted! I guess if you have worked your way through the book trying the combos, you may well be in need of losing a couple of pounds, or Kilograms if your have gone all metric.. I guess that also I need to cater for all needs including the stick thin gym junkies out there! So here it is, I can't believe I have included it, the diet one.

Prep your single fish finger, take out your nimble style bread, I don't recommend that you toast it as it tends to disintegrate.. Apply your cottage cheese and lettuce leaf, place on the fish finger and top of with another slice of diet bread. Yuk.

That's your lot, but as I am sure all of you are aware, there are possibly millions of different combo's that were have not explored in the book. For those of you that would like to see something that you have created in the next book, then drop me a line at jasondearn@yahoo.co.uk entitling it "butty ideas" and you never know I might get around to writing another volume, (I already have the book cover design – two fish fingers instead of one!). Any included combo's will get the creators name in print – alas no royalties I'm afraid, I need shoes!

Thanks guys

Jase,

Worcestershire, Jan – Dec 2010.

Update:

It is Sunday morning. I have just gotten up to survey the damage from last night's alcohol intake when I found it! The sneak, there is a pickled egg on the coffee table! Arrgh!!

Printed in Great Britain
by Amazon

59426595R00047